SOCIAL WELFARE

Contents

Social Welfare

London: H M S O

Researched and written by Reference Services, Central Office of Information.

This publication is an expanded and updated version of the chapter on social welfare which appears in *Britain 1993: An Official Handbook*.

ISBN 0 11 701732 9

HMSO publications are available from:

HMSO Publications Centre
(Mail, fax and telephone orders only)
PO Box 276, London SW8 5DT
Telephone orders 071-873 9090
General enquiries 071-873 0011
(queuing system in operation for both numbers)
Fax orders 071-873 8200

HMSO Bookshops
49 High Holborn, London WC1V 6HB   071-873 0011
Fax 071-873 8200 (counter service only)
258 Broad Street, Birmingham B1 2HE   021-643 3740   Fax 021-643 6510
Southey House, 33 Wine Street, Bristol BS1 2BQ
0272 264306   Fax 0272 294515
9-21 Princess Street, Manchester M60 8AS   061-834 7201   Fax 061-833 0634
16 Arthur Street, Belfast BT1 4GD   0232 238451   Fax 0232 235401
71 Lothian Road, Edinburgh EH3 9AZ   031-228 4181   Fax 031-229 2734

HMSO's Accredited Agents
(see Yellow Pages)

and through good booksellers

Cover Photograph Credits
Top: Women's Royal Voluntary Service; left: National Blood Transfusion Service; right: Sally and Richard Greenhill.

Introduction

Britain's[1] social welfare system comprises the National Health Service, personal social services and the social security programme. This book outlines the organisation and functions of the three services, describes recent developments in each area and covers government policies towards them.

More detailed accounts of individual aspects of the social welfare system will be available in forthcoming titles in the Aspects of Britain series. These will include health promotion, AIDS control, and care of elderly and disabled people.

Further information on developments in social welfare is contained in *Current Affairs—A Monthly Survey*, published by HMSO.

---

[1] 'Britain' is used informally in this book to mean the United Kingdom of Great Britain and Northern Ireland; Great Britain comprises England, Scotland and Wales.

Historical Outline

The earliest social welfare services in Britain were provided by various religious orders, augmented in medieval times by the manor houses and merchant and craft guilds, which assumed as part of their duties and responsibilities the care of the sick and the destitute. This practice fell into disuse with the decay of the feudal system and the dissolution of the monasteries. By the end of the sixteenth century it had become imperative to find some substitute for the old system. In 1601, therefore, the *Poor Relief Act* gave local government authorities in England and Wales the duty to provide from local taxation for the sick, the needy, and the homeless. (A similar Act had been passed in Scotland in 1579.) Local authorities also began to take some steps to control water supplies and to try to check epidemics.

In the eighteenth and nineteenth centuries British medical services developed. Medical science advanced and the number of qualified doctors greatly increased. Hospitals were built with private endowments and subscriptions and were made increasingly available on a charitable basis to the general population, while free 'infirmaries' were provided under the Poor Law for the destitute, aged and infirm. From the middle of the nineteenth century working people of modest means began increasingly to insure against periods of illness by subscribing to provident and friendly societies and sick clubs. Many public-spirited medical practitioners would at that time remit all or most of their fees to the poor.

Public measures to promote healthier living conditions, however, preceded adequate public provision for the care of the sick.

Rapid growth of towns in the first half of the nineteenth century caused an intensification of sanitary problems with consequent cholera, typhoid and other epidemics. A programme of sanitary reform, associated particularly with Edwin Chadwick (1800–90), Secretary to the Poor Law Commission, led to the passage of the *Public Health Act 1848* which, for the first time, established a comprehensive public health system under unified control and laid down minimum standards for its services. The system was further developed and consolidated by the *Public Health Act 1875,* upon which all subsequent health legislation has been based.

In the twentieth century the provision for personal health services began to improve rapidly as the result of the progress of medical knowledge and the wider availability of treatment. *The National Health Insurance Act 1911* introduced a scheme whereby all people earning wages less than £160 a year (later raised to £420) were entitled to the services of a general practitioner in return for regular contributions made by themselves and their employers to certain insurance organisations, known as approved societies. The doctors who took part were paid a capitation fee for the patients who had asked to be on their list and been accepted. This scheme came to cover most of the poorer half of the population while the rest were dependent for their medical care either on paying fees as private patients, or on a certain number of voluntary sick clubs (a form of voluntary insurance whereby people paid the doctor a few pence a week).

At the same time the voluntary hospitals expanded their free services for the poor with the aid of voluntary donations and contributions and the fees of other patients. After 1929 the Poor Law Infirmaries began to develop into local authority general hospitals. Some local authorities began to provide improved social and health services, mainly for schools, mothers and children.

These various health services, however, were unevenly distributed and were seen to be inadequate. Proposals for a full health and medical service were the subject of many reports in the interwar years; it was, however, the second world war which precipitated reform in this, as in many other matters. To deal with the war wounded, the Emergency Hospital Service, including both voluntary and municipal hospitals, was developed within existing organisations as required. The welfare food service for mothers was introduced and school meals services and industrial canteens were expanded.

The Beveridge Report

In 1941 an inter-departmental committee was set up under Sir William (later Lord) Beveridge to conduct a survey of the existing national schemes of social insurance and allied services and to make recommendations on the way that social services should be reconstructed after the end of the war. The committee's report, known as the Beveridge Report, was published in 1942; it recommended far-reaching changes involving a considerable extension of both the health and social security services and formed the basis of much post-war social legislation. In 1943 the wartime all-party Government announced its acceptance of the proposal in the Beveridge Report that a comprehensive health service for all purposes and all people should be established. The first plan for a comprehensive national health service was published by the Government in 1944. The final plan was embodied in the *National Health Service Act 1946*, and the National Health Service started on 5 July 1948. This provided a complete general practitioner and hospital service for the community, and expanded the preventive social and environmental services provided by local authorities.

Britain was thus the first country in the world to offer free medical care to the whole population. Many other countries had developed compulsory health insurance schemes, but under them rights to health care were generally confined to those who had paid contributions and their dependants, and to pensioners. The principle of *universal* coverage for free medical care was entirely new.

The Services Today

The National Health Service (NHS) provides a full range of medical services which are available to all residents, regardless of their income. Local authority personal social services and voluntary organisations provide help and advice to the most vulnerable members of the community. These include elderly, physically disabled and mentally ill people, those with learning disabilities (mental handicap) and children in need of care. The social security system is designed to secure a basic standard of living for people in financial need by providing income during periods of inability to earn (including periods of unemployment), help for families and assistance with costs arising from disablement.

Central government is directly responsible for the NHS, administered by a range of local health authorities and boards throughout Britain acting as its agents, and for the social security system. Personal social services are administered by local authorities but central government is responsible for establishing national policies, issuing guidance and overseeing standards. Joint finance and planning between health and local authorities aims to prevent overlapping of services and to encourage the development of community services.

Planned spending on social welfare in 1992–93 is: health, over £34,000 million, and social security benefits (the Government's largest expenditure programme) over £68,000 million, while the standard spending assessment for personal social services is over £5,000 million.

Spending on the health service has increased substantially in real terms since 1980, and is planned to grow further over the next two years. More patients are being treated than ever before. Spending on social security is rising because of increased numbers of beneficiaries, especially retirement pensioners, and the long-term sick and disabled. The value of retirement and most other long-term benefits has also increased in real terms since 1980. Spending on the personal social services is determined by local authorities. Central government has restricted the total expenditure of individual local authorities, but spending has risen substantially in real terms since the late 1970s, reflecting the priority given to this sector.

In England the NHS health programme consists of:

—Hospital and Community Health Services (HCHS), providing all hospital care and a range of community health services;

—Family Health Services (FHS), providing general medical, dental and pharmaceutical services and some ophthalmic services, and covering the cost of most medicines prescribed by general practitioners (GPs);

—Central Health and Miscellaneous Services (CHMS), providing services most effectively administered centrally, such as welfare food and support to the voluntary sector; and

—the administrative costs of the Department of Health.

Major Policy Developments

Major Reforms in Management

The NHS and Community Care Act 1990 introduced wide-ranging reform in management and patient care in the health and social care services.

Health Service Expenditure in England

NHS Gross Expenditure 1991–92 (estimate)

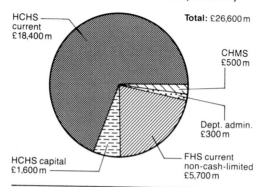

HCHS current £18,400 m

Total: £26,600 m

CHMS £500 m

Dept. admin. £300 m

FHS current non-cash-limited £5,700 m

HCHS capital £1,600 m

Hospital and Community Health Services Gross Current Expenditure by Sector 1989–90 (estimate)

Total: £13,466 m

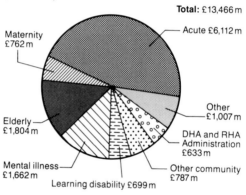

Maternity £762 m

Acute £6,112 m

Other £1,007 m

DHA and RHA Administration £633 m

Elderly £1,804 m

Mental illness £1,662 m

Learning disability £699 m

Other community £787 m

1. Other community services include health visiting, immunisation, screening, health promotion and community dental services.

Non-cash-limited Family Health Services Gross Expenditure 1990–91

Total: £5,287 m

Pharmaceutical services £2,652 m

General ophthalmic services £111 m

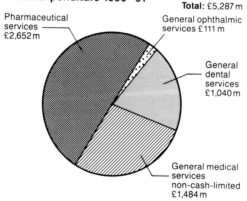

General dental services £1,040 m

General medical services non-cash-limited £1,484 m

Source: Department of Health. The Government's Expenditure Plans 1992–93 to 1994–95.

The NHS reforms came into effect in April 1991. Their aim is to give patients, wherever they live in Britain, better health care and greater choice of service.

—Health authorities have been given a new role as purchasers of health care on behalf of their local residents and are responsible for assessing local health care needs and ensuring the availability of a full range of services to meet identified health needs. They ensure that those needs are met within existing resources.

—Each health authority is funded to buy health care for its local residents through arranging contracts with hospitals and other health service units in either the public or private sector. For the first time hospitals are directly funded for the number of patients they treat, making it easier for GPs to refer patients outside their area if treatment elsewhere is faster and better. However, powers exist for allocating resources where the urgent need for treatment does not allow NHS contracts to be arranged in advance.

—The contracts agreed between health authorities and hospitals set out the quality, quantity and cost of the services to be delivered during the year. The contracts secured by each health authority are based on wide consultation with all local GPs.

—Hospitals may apply to become self-governing NHS trusts (see p. 24), independent of local health authority control but remaining within the NHS, accountable to the relevant health department, treating NHS patients, and funded largely through general taxation, through contracts with health authorities.

—GPs from larger medical practices may apply to join the general practitioner fundholding scheme (see p. 20), under which they receive an annual budget directly from the health authority, enabling them to buy certain hospital services for their patients. The reforms in community care provision, which take effect between April 1991 and April 1993, establish a new financial and managerial framework which aims to secure the delivery of good quality services in line with national objectives. They are intended to enable vulnerable groups in the community to live as independently as possible in their own homes for as long as they are able and wish to do so, and to give them a greater say in how they live and how the services they need should be provided. (For fuller details see p. 54.)

Broadly similar changes have been introduced under separate legislation in Northern Ireland, where health and personal social services are provided on an integrated basis by health and social services boards.

The Patient's Charter

The Patient's Charter, published in 1991, is part of the health departments' contribution to the Citizen's Charter White Paper, a government initiative designed to raise standards of service and to make providers of all the public services fully accountable to the users of those services.[2] The Patient's Charter shares the objectives of the NHS reforms: to improve standards of health care and sensitivity to patients in the NHS. It sets out for the first time the rights of patients and the standards of care they can expect to receive from the NHS. The Government believes that patients should know what they can expect from the NHS and that the staff who provide services should understand what is expected of them.

[2] For further details see *The British System of Government* (Aspects of Britain: HMSO, 1992).

The responsibility for implementing the Patient's Charter rests with health authorities.

As well as restating the existing rights that patients have under the NHS, the Patient's Charter sets out three new rights introduced in April 1992. These are that patients must:

— be given detailed information on local health services, including quality standards and maximum waiting times;

— be guaranteed admission for treatment no later than two years from the date of being placed on a waiting list; and

— have any complaint about NHS services investigated, and receive a full reply as soon as possible.

The Patient's Charter also sets national charter standards. These are not legal rights but specific standards of service which the NHS aims to provide. These cover respect for the individual patient, waiting times for ambulances, assessment in casualty departments, appointments in outpatient clinics, and cancellation of operations. Also included are local charter standards of service which health authorities aim to provide.

Separate Patient's Charters have been developed for Scotland, Wales and Northern Ireland.

Developing Health Strategies

The Government emphasises the importance of promoting health as well as treating illness. Preventive health services such as health education, and the responsibility that individuals have for their own health, play a major part in this. While great progress has been made in eliminating infectious diseases such as poliomyelitis and tuberculosis, there is still scope for greater success in controlling the major causes of early death and disability.

The White Paper *The Health of the Nation,* published in July 1992, sets out a strategy for improving health. This is the first time a strategy has been developed for health in England and its long-term aim is to enable people to live longer, healthier lives. It sets targets for improvements in the following areas:

—coronary heart disease and stroke (the major cause of premature death in England);

—cancers (the second biggest cause of premature death);

—accidents (the commonest cause of death in those under 30);

—mental illness (a leading cause of ill-health and, through suicides, of death); and

—HIV/AIDS and sexual health (HIV/AIDS is perhaps the greatest new public health threat this century—see p. 40—and there is much scope for reducing sexually transmitted diseases and unwanted pregnancies).

Targets are set for reducing death rates (for example, from coronary heart disease and stroke in those under 65 by at least 40 per cent by the year 2000), for reducing ill-health (such as the incidence of invasive cervical cancer by at least 20 per cent by 2000) and for reducing risk behaviour (for example, the percentage of smokers to no more than 20 per cent of the population by the year 2000). While the NHS will have a central role in working towards the targets, the strategy also emphasises that there is a role for everyone in improving the nation's health. Progress towards these targets will be monitored, and the strategy will be reviewed periodically with a view to adding further areas.

The White Paper also sets out the Government's objective of ensuring the provision of effective family planning services for those people who want them. The conception rate for those under 16 years is a matter of particular concern.

Strategies have also been developed for Scotland, Wales and Northern Ireland.

National Health Service

The NHS is based upon the principle that there should be a full range of publicly provided services designed to help the individual stay healthy. The services are intended to provide effective and appropriate treatment and care where necessary while making the best use of available resources. All taxpayers, employers and employees contribute to its cost so that those members of the community who do not require health care help to pay for those who do. Some forms of treatment, such as hospital care, are provided free; others (see p. 16) may be charged for.

Growth in real spending on the health service is being used to meet the needs of increasing numbers of elderly people and to take full advantage of advances in medical technology. It is also used to provide more appropriate types of care, often in the community rather than in hospital, for priority groups such as the elderly, the mentally ill and people with learning disabilities (mental handicap). Increased spending has, in addition, been allocated to combat the growing health problems arising from alcohol and drug misuse; and to remedy disparities in provision between the regions of Britain.

The Government stresses the need for a partnership between the public and private health sectors and for improving efficiency in order to secure the best value for money and the maximum patient care. Measures to achieve more effective management of resources in the NHS have included:

—appointing at regional, district and unit levels general managers drawn from inside and outside the health service;

—improving the accountability of health authorities for the planning and management of their resources;

—increasing the proportion of total staff who provide direct patient care, such as doctors and nurses; and

—introducing a range of programmes to provide services at lower cost.

Considerable savings have been made through competitive tendering for hospital cleaning, catering and laundry services. At the end of 1991 the Government announced that total annual savings from competitive tendering amounted to £156 million. Economies are also made in prescribing by restricting the use of expensive branded products in favour of cheaper but equally effective equivalent medicines.

Administration

The Secretary of State for Health in England and the Secretaries of State for Scotland, Wales and Northern Ireland are responsible for all aspects of the health services in their respective countries. The Department of Health is responsible for national strategic planning in England. The Scottish Office Home and Health Department, the Welsh Office and the Department of Health and Social Services in Northern Ireland have similar responsibilities.

District health authorities in England and Wales and health boards in Scotland are responsible for securing hospital and community health services in their areas. England, because of its greater size and population, also has regional authorities responsible for regional planning, resource allocation, major capital building work and certain specialised hospital services best administered on a regional basis. The authorities and boards co-operate closely with local authorities responsible for social work, environmental health, education and other services. Family health services authorities (health boards in Scotland) arrange for the provision of services by doctors, dentists, pharmacists and opticians, as well as administering their contracts. Community health councils (local health councils in Scotland) represent local opinion on the health services provided.

In Northern Ireland health and social services boards are responsible for all health and personal social services in their areas. The representation of public opinion on these services is provided for by area health and social services councils.

Finance

Over 80 per cent of the cost of the health service in Great Britain is paid for through general taxation. The rest is met from the NHS element of National Insurance contributions—which are paid by employed people, their employers, and self-employed people—and from charges towards the cost of certain items such as drugs prescribed by family doctors, and general dental treatment. Health authorities may raise funds from voluntary sources. Certain hospitals increase their revenue by taking private patients who pay the full cost of their accommodation and treatment.

Almost 80 per cent of medical prescription items are supplied free. Prescription charges do not apply to the following:

—children under 16 years (or students under 19 and still in full-time education);

—expectant mothers and women who have had a baby in the last year;

—women aged 60 and over and men aged 65 and over;

—patients suffering from certain medical conditions;

—war and armed forces disablement pensioners (for prescriptions which relate to the disability for which they receive a war pension); and

—people who are receiving income support or family credit (see pp. 81–2); and people or families with low incomes.

There are proportional charges for all types of general dental treatment, including dental examination. However, women who were pregnant when the dentist accepted them for treatment or who have had a baby in the last year, anyone under the age of 18 (or 19 if in full-time education), people receiving income support or family credit, and families on low incomes do not have to pay. Sight tests are free to children, those on low incomes and certain other priority groups. Some disadvantaged groups receive help with the purchase, repair and replacement of spectacles.

Hospital medical staffs are salaried and may be employed full time or part time. Family practitioners (doctors, dentists, opticians and pharmacists) are self-employed and have contracts with the NHS. GPs are paid by a system of fees and allowances designed to reflect responsibilities, workload and practice expenses. Dentists providing treatment in their own surgeries are paid by a combination of capitation fees for treating children, continuing care payments for adults registered with the practice, and a prescribed scale of fees for individual treatments. Pharmacists dispensing from their own premises are refunded the cost of the items supplied, together with professional fees. Ophthalmic medical practitioners and ophthalmic opticians taking part in the general ophthalmic service receive approved fees for each sight test carried out.

Staffing

The NHS is one of the largest employers in the world, with a work-force of nearly one million people. During the last ten years there has been a rise in the numbers of 'direct care staff' and a corresponding fall in the numbers of support staff. The fall in the numbers of directly employed ancillary staff and of maintenance and works staff reflects the results of competitive tendering. Staff costs account for two-thirds of total NHS expenditure and 70 per cent of current expenditure on hospitals and community health services. In England between 1981 and 1990:

—the number of hospital medical consultants increased from 12,400 to 15,200;

—the number of junior hospital doctors increased from 20,800 to 23,500;

—the number of hospital dental staff rose to 2,100;

—the number of nursing and midwifery staff, who make up 50 per cent of the workforce, increased by 2.6 per cent (including agency staff); and

—the number of scientific, professional and technical staff rose by 20 per cent.

Health Service Commissioners

There are three posts of Health Service Commissioner (one each for England, Scotland and Wales) for dealing with complaints from members of the public about the health service. The three posts are held by the same person, who is also the Parliamentary Commissioner for Administration (Ombudsman), who reports annually to Parliament. The Health Service Commissioner can investigate complaints that a health authority, NHS trust or family health services authority has not carried out its statutory duties, has provided an inadequate service or, through maladministration, has caused injustice or hardship.

Complaints about clinical judgment, GPs, personnel matters and the use of a health authority's discretionary powers lie beyond the Health Service Commissioner's jurisdiction, and separate procedures exist for these. In Northern Ireland the Commissioner for Complaints has a similar role.

Family Health Services

The family health services are those given to patients by doctors, dentists, opticians and pharmacists of their own choice. GPs provide the first diagnosis in the case of illness and either prescribe a suitable course of treatment or refer a patient to the more specialised services and hospital consultants.

About four-fifths of GPs in Britain work in partnerships or group practices, often as members of primary health-care teams. The teams also include health visitors and district nurses, and sometimes midwives, social workers and other professional staff employed by the health authorities. About a quarter of GPs in Great Britain and about half in Northern Ireland work in modern and well-equipped health centres, where medical and nursing services are provided. Health centres may also have facilities for health education, family planning, speech therapy, chiropody, assessment of hearing, physiotherapy and remedial exercises. Dental, pharmaceutical and ophthalmic services, hospital outpatient and supporting social work services may also be provided.

There have been substantial increases in primary health care staff in recent years. For example, in England and Wales between

1980 and 1991, the number of GPs increased by 18 per cent (to 29,700), and average patient list size fell by 13 per cent (to 1,900), while the number of family dentists increased by 26 per cent (to 16,400). The number of GP practice nurses has increased more than tenfold—from 900 in 1978 to 9,950 in 1991.

Special funds have been earmarked by the Government for improving the quality of primary health care in inner city areas. Efforts have also been made to improve health services for black and other ethnic minority groups. These include new health projects in Britain's Chinese communities, and increased central funding for health information material to be produced in many minority languages.

The Government has welcomed a recent report which recommends ways in which the role of community pharmacists could be developed to increase their contribution to health care.

Eye Services

Entitlement to free NHS sight tests is restricted to people on low incomes, children and those with particular medical needs. Spectacles are supplied by registered ophthalmic and dispensing opticians but unregistered retailers may also sell spectacles to most adults. Children, people on low incomes and those requiring certain complex lenses receive a voucher to put towards the cost of their spectacles.

Recent Developments

GP Fundholders

Under the NHS and Community Care Act 1990 GP practices with 9,000 patients or over may apply for fundholding status. (From

April 1993 this figure will fall to 7,000 patients.) This is a voluntary scheme which gives larger medical practices the opportunity to manage sums of NHS money for the benefit of their patients. It aims to improve services for patients and enable GPs to explore more innovative methods of providing health care. GP fundholders are responsible for part of their own NHS budgets, enabling them to buy certain non-urgent hospital services. Prescription charges and part of the cost of running the practice are also covered. Fundholders may negotiate for services directly with hospitals from both public and private sectors in any district or regional health authority in Britain. By April 1992 over 3,000 GPs in about 600 practices in England had become fundholders, covering nearly 6.7 million people, or 14 per cent of the population. A further 2,500 GPs in some 600 practices are preparing to join the scheme in April 1993. From April 1993 the scheme will be expanded to enable GP fundholders to buy district nursing and health visiting services from NHS community units.

Contracts

A new performance-related contract for GPs came into effect in 1990, the first major reform of the family doctor service for over 20 years. It is designed to raise standards of care, extend the range of services available to patients and improve patient choice. The changes are intended to make it easier for patients to see their GP at times convenient to them and easier for patients to change doctors; and to encourage doctors to practise more preventive medicine.

A new contract for dentists was introduced in 1990 aimed at improving care and providing more information to patients about general dental services. As a result NHS dental care now includes preventive care as well as restorative treatment. All adult patients are now offered 'continuing care', and dentists are encouraged to practise more preventive dentistry for children. There are also incentives for dentists to undertake further training.

Medical Audit

Medical audit, which is the systematic, critical analysis by doctors at all levels in the health service of the quality of the medical care they give their patients, including the procedures used for diagnosis and treatment, the use of resources and the resulting outcome, has been introduced in all health authorities. In 1991–92 the Government allocated £46 million to continue to develop medical audit in the hospital and community health services.

Health Visitors, District Nurses and Midwives

Health visitors are responsible for the preventive care and health education of families, particularly those with young children. They work closely with GPs, district nurses and other professions. District nurses give skilled nursing care to people at home or elsewhere outside hospital; they also play an important role in health promotion and education. Although almost all babies are born in hospital, some antenatal care and most postnatal care is given in the community by midwives and GPs, who also care for women having their babies at home. Midwives are responsible for educating and supporting women and their families during pregnancy and childbirth.

Hospital and Specialist Services

A full range of hospital services is provided by district general hospitals. These include treatment and diagnostic facilities for inpatients, day patients and outpatients; maternity departments; infectious disease units; psychiatric and geriatric facilities; rehabilitation facilities; and other forms of specialised treatment. There are also specialist hospitals or units for children, people suffering from mental illness, those with learning disabilities, and elderly people, and for the treatment of specific diseases. Examples of these include the world-famous Hospital for Sick Children, Great Ormond Street, and the Brompton Heart and Chest Hospital in London. Hospitals designated as teaching hospitals combine treatment facilities with training medical and other students, and research work.

Many of the hospitals in the NHS were built in the nineteenth century; some, such as St Bartholomew's and St Thomas's in London, trace their origins to much earlier charitable foundations.

Much has been done to improve and extend existing hospital buildings and many new hospitals have been, or are being opened.

Since 1979 in Great Britain over 600 health building schemes, each costing £1 million or more, have been completed. A further 400 schemes are at various stages of development. This is the largest sustained building programme in the history of the NHS.

Recent policy in England and Wales has been to provide a balanced hospital service centred around a district general hospital, complemented as necessary by smaller, locally based hospitals and facilities.

A new development in hospital planning in England and Wales is the nucleus hospital. This is designed to accommodate a full range of district general hospital facilities and is capable of being built in self-contained phases or as an extension to an existing hospital. By mid-1992, 83 nucleus hospitals had been completed. A further 56 are at various stages of construction or planning. Those already open have proved economical to build and are providing high-quality and cost-effective services to patients.

The world's first low-energy nucleus hospital, which is expected to use less than half the energy of a conventional nucleus hospital, opened on the Isle of Wight in 1991, and another is being built in Northumberland.

The hospital service is now treating more patients a year than ever before. Between 1979 and 1990–91 lengths of stay for in-patients declined and the number of people treated as day patients more than doubled. Newer forms of treatment and diagnosis are being made more widely available. These include kidney dialysis, hip replacements, laser treatment and body scanning.

In 1986 the Government launched a drive to reduce hospital waiting lists and times. In 1992–93 £39 million is being invested in a variety of projects, including mobile operating theatres, to improve waiting times for patients. Preliminary figures show that the number of patients waiting between one and two years for treatment fell by nearly 40,000 or 33 per cent while the total waiting list dropped by over 33,000 or 3.5 per cent in 1991–92.

Community services such as the psychiatric nursing service, day hospitals, and local authority day centres have expanded so that more patients remain in the community and others are sent home from hospital sooner.

NHS Trusts

Under the NHS and Community Care Act 1990 hospitals and other health service units (for example, ambulance services and community health services) may apply to become independent of local health authority control and establish themselves as self-governing NHS trusts. These are run by boards of directors, and are free to employ their own staff and set their own rates of pay, carry out research and provide facilities for medical education and other forms of training. Self-governing NHS trusts derive their income mainly from NHS contracts to provide services to health authorities and GP fundholders. The trusts may treat private patients. All trusts must provide annual reports, and annual accounts modelled on commercial accountancy practices. By August 1992, 156 NHS trusts had been established.

Private Medical Treatment

The Government's policy is for the NHS and the independent sector to co-operate in meeting the nation's health needs. It believes that this will benefit the NHS by adding to the resources devoted to health care and offering flexibility to health authorities in the delivery of services. Some health authorities share expensive facilities and equipment with private hospitals, and NHS patients are sometimes treated (at public expense) in the private sector to reduce waiting lists. The scale of private practice in relation to the NHS is, however, small.

It is estimated that about three-quarters of those receiving acute treatment in private hospitals or NHS hospital pay-beds are covered by health insurance schemes, which make provision for private health care in return for annual subscriptions. Over 3 million people subscribe to such schemes, half of them within group schemes, some arranged by firms on behalf of employees. Subscriptions often cover more than one person (for example, members of a family) and the total number of people covered by private medical insurance in Britain is estimated at over 6 million. The Government has introduced tax relief on private health insurance premiums paid by people aged 60 and over to encourage the increased use of private health facilities.

Many overseas patients come to Britain for treatment in private hospitals and clinics, and Harley Street in London is an internationally recognised centre for medical consultancy.

There is a growing interest in alternative therapies such as homoeopathy, osteopathy and acupuncture, which are mainly practised outside the NHS.

Organ Transplants

Over the past 25 years there have been significant developments in transplant surgery in Britain. The United Kingdom Transplant Support Service Authority provides a centralised organ matching and distribution service. During 1991, 1,690 kidney transplants were performed. A similar service exists for corneas, and in 1991, 2,226 were transplanted.

Heart transplant operations have been conducted at Papworth Hospital in Cambridgeshire and Harefield Hospital in London since 1979. There are six other heart transplant centres in England, while Scotland's first unit opened in Glasgow in late 1991.

A programme of combined heart and lung transplants is in progress and in 1991 over 280 heart and 81 heart–lung transplants were performed. The world's first combined heart, lungs and liver transplant operation was carried out at Papworth in 1987.

There are six liver transplant units in England and 419 liver transplants were performed in 1991. Scotland's first liver transplant centre opened in Edinburgh in November 1992. A voluntary organ donor card system enables people to indicate their willingness to become organ donors in the event of their death. Commercial dealing in organs for transplant is illegal.

Blood Transfusion

The blood transfusion service in England and Wales collects over 2 million donations of blood and over 133,700 donations of plasma each year from voluntary unpaid donors; in Scotland the figures are over 350,000 and over 18,000 respectively. Regional transfusion centres recruit donors and organise donor sessions in towns and villages, factories and offices, and within the armed forces. Donors are normally aged between 18 and 65. The centres are also responsible for blood grouping and testing, maintaining blood banks, providing a consultancy service to hospitals, teaching in medical schools, and instructing doctors, nurses and technicians. The Central Blood Laboratories Authority is responsible for the manufacture of blood products as well as for research. There is also increasing emphasis on the most effective use of blood and, in particular, its separation into components such as plasma for specific uses. A laboratory at Elstree, Hertfordshire, was opened in 1987 with the aim of meeting the needs for all blood products in England and Wales. Facilities in Scotland are being expanded to cope with rising demand.

Ambulance and Patient Transport Services

NHS emergency ambulances are available free of charge for cases of sudden illness or collapse, and for doctors' urgent calls. Rapid response services, in which paramedics use cars and motor cycles to reach emergency cases, have been introduced in a number of areas, particularly London and other major cities with areas of high traffic density. Helicopter ambulances serve many parts of England and in Scotland an air ambulance service is available in the islands and the remoter parts of the mainland.

Non-emergency patient transport services are available to NHS patients considered by their doctor (or dentist or midwife) to be medically unfit to travel by other means. The principle applied is that each patient should be able to reach hospital in a reasonable time and in reasonable comfort, without detriment to his or her medical condition. In many areas the ambulance service organises volunteer drivers to provide a hospital car service for non-urgent patients.

Rehabilitation

Rehabilitation begins at the onset of illness or of injury and continues throughout, with the aim of helping people to adjust to changes in lifestyle and to live as normally as possible. Rehabilitation services are available for elderly, young, disabled and mentally ill people, and those with learning disabilities who need such help to resume life in the community. These services are offered in hospitals, centres in the community and in people's own homes through co-ordinated work by a range of professional workers.

Medical services may provide free artificial limbs and eyes, hearing aids, surgical supports, wheelchairs, and other appliances. Following assessment, very severely physically handicapped patients may be provided with environmental control equipment which enables them to operate devices such as alarm bells, radios and televisions, telephones, and heating appliances. Nursing aids may be provided on loan for use in the home.

Local authorities may provide a range of facilities to help patients in the transition from hospital to their own homes. These include the provision of aids, care from home helps, and professional help from occupational therapists and social workers.

Voluntary organisations also provide help, complementing the work of the statutory agencies and widening the range of services.

Hospices

A number of hospices provide care for terminally ill people (including children), either directly in inpatient or day-care units or through nursing and other assistance in the patient's own home. Control of symptoms and psychological support for patients and their families form central features of the modern hospice movement, which started in Britain and is now worldwide. Some hospices are administered entirely by the NHS; the remainder are run by independent charities, some receiving support from public funds. The number of voluntary hospices has more than doubled in the past ten years; there are now over 100 inpatient units providing over 1,900 beds, and more than 150 day-care units offering some 1,500 places.

The Government is seeking to provide a level of public funding for the hospice movement which matches voluntary donations. In 1992–93, £31.7 million is being allocated to health authorities to enable them to offer increased support to hospices and similar organisations, while a further £5.5 million has been allocated to enable them to arrange for drugs to be supplied to hospices without charge. The National Council for Hospice and Specialist Palliative Care Services was launched in February 1992.

Parents and Children

Special preventive services are provided under the health service to safeguard the health of expectant mothers and of mothers with young children. Services include free dental treatment, dried milk and vitamins; health education; and vaccination and immunisation of children against certain infectious diseases (see p. 43). Pregnant women receive antenatal care from their GPs and hospital clinics, and women in paid employment have the right to visit the clinics during working hours. Some 99 per cent of women have their babies in hospital, returning home shortly afterwards to be attended by a midwife or health visitor and, where necessary, their GP.

The Government attaches great importance to improving the quality of maternity services, and to making them more responsive to women's wishes on how care is provided. The perinatal mortality rate (the number of stillbirths and deaths in the first week of life) has fallen in England and Wales from 14.7 per 1,000 births in 1979 to 8 per 1,000 births in 1991—its lowest recorded level. Similar reductions have occurred in Scotland and Northern Ireland.

A comprehensive programme of health surveillance is provided for pre-school children in clinics run by the community health authorities, and increasingly by GPs. This enables doctors, dentists and health visitors to oversee the physical and mental health and development of pre-school children. Information on preventive services is given and welfare foods are distributed. The school health service offers health care and advice for schoolchildren, including medical and dental inspection and treatment where necessary. Child guidance and child psychiatric services provide help and advice for children with psychological or emotional problems.

In recent years special efforts have been made to improve co-operation between the community-based child health services and local authority social services for children. This is particularly important in the prevention of child abuse and for the health and welfare of children in care.

Human Fertilisation and Embryology

The world's first 'test-tube baby' was born in Britain in 1978, as a result of the technique of *in vitro* fertilisation. This opened up new horizons for helping with problems of infertility and for the science of embryology. The social, ethical and legal implications were examined by a committee of inquiry under Baroness Warnock, which reported in 1984. There was general consultation on the Warnock Report and government policy was set out in a White Paper in 1987, which was followed by the Human Fertilisation and Embryology Act 1990. The Act provided for:

—the establishment of the Human Fertilisation and Embryology Authority (HFEA) to control and license centres providing certain infertility treatments, and centres undertaking human embryo research and storage of gametes and embryos;

—research to be permitted on embryos for up to 14 days after fertilisation;

—the legal status and rights of children born as a result of *in vitro* fertilisation and techniques involving donation; and

—the clarification of the legal position on surrogate motherhood (the practice where one woman bears a child for another).

The HFEA maintains a code of practice giving guidance about licensed centres and must report annually to Parliament.

These provisions constitute one of the most comprehensive pieces of legislation on assisted reproduction and embryo research in the world.

Legislation to ban commercial surrogacy agencies, and advertising of or for surrogacy services, was passed in 1985.

Family Planning

Free family planning advice and treatment are available to women from family doctors and from health authority family planning clinics, which also make services available to men. Family planning is one of the key areas covered by the White Paper *The Health of the Nation* (see p. 12).

Abortion

The Abortion Act 1967, as amended in 1990, allows the ending of a pregnancy of up to 24 weeks by a doctor if two doctors consider that continuing the pregnancy would involve greater risk of injury to the physical or mental health of the woman (or to any existing children of the family) than having an abortion. There are three categories in which no time limit applies: where there is a risk of grave permanent injury to the physical or mental health of the woman; where there is a substantial risk of foetal handicap; or where continuing the pregnancy would involve a risk to the life of the pregnant woman greater than that of the pregnancy being terminated.

The Act does not apply in Northern Ireland.

Drug Misuse

The misuse of dangerous drugs, such as heroin, cocaine and amphetamines, is a serious social and health problem, and the Government has made the fight against such misuse a major priority. Its strategy comprises action to reduce the supply of illicit drugs from abroad; to promote more effective law enforcement by the police and Customs services; and to maintain tight controls on medicinal drugs that can be misused. It also includes action to maintain effective deterrents against misuse; to develop effective programmes to treat and rehabilitate misusers; and to prevent people who are not misusers from starting, by means of educational programmes and publicity campaigns.

Research on various aspects of drug misuse is funded by several government departments. The Government is advised on a wide range of matters relating to drug misuse and connected social problems by the Advisory Council on the Misuse of Drugs.

Drug Statistics

Recent drug statistics show that between 1990 and 1991:

— the number of notified drug addicts increased by 17 per cent (to 21,000);

— the proportion addicted to heroin fell from 80 per cent to 70 per cent; those reported to be dependent on methadone increased from 30 per cent to 40 per cent (this figure includes those receiving methadone by prescription as part of a course of treatment); under 10 per cent were reported to be addicted to cocaine; and

— the proportion of addicts injecting drugs fell from 65 per cent to 59 per cent.

Prevention

The Government began a major national publicity campaign in 1985 to persuade young people not to take drugs, and to advise parents, teachers and other professionals on how to recognise and combat the problem. Subsequent phases of the campaign have warned of the dangers of heroin misuse and of the risks of transmitting HIV, the virus which causes AIDS (see p. 40), through the sharing of injecting equipment. In 1991–92 the focus of the campaign changed to give greater emphasis to locally-based campaigns; the total cost of the campaign was £4 million.

The Drug Prevention Initiative has provided funding for the establishment of local drug prevention teams in 20 areas in England, Scotland and Wales. Their task is to strengthen community resistance to drug misuse. The total budget for the initiative is £5.5 million in 1992–93. Separate measures have been introduced in Scotland to discourage drug misuse through publicity campaigns and action in the education service and the community.

The Government continues to make funds available for local education authorities in England and Wales to appoint staff to promote and co-ordinate preventive work in their areas, especially for anti-drug misuse work in schools. As part of the National Curriculum, children in primary and secondary schools receive education on the dangers of drug misuse.

Treatment and Rehabilitation

A total of £17.5 million over the three years 1988–89 to 1990–91 was spent on the development of services for drug misusers. Additional sums have been made available since 1986–87 through the health authorities in England for the expansion of services for drug misusers, rising to nearly £17.2 million in 1992–93. A further grant of £2.1 million in 1992–93 is intended to help local authorities to develop voluntary sector services for drug as well as alcohol misusers. Similar projects are in progress in Wales and in Scotland, where over £2 million is made available annually to health boards for the support of drug misuse services. To reduce the spread of AIDS a number of trial schemes are in progress, offering drug misusers counselling and the exchange of clean for used syringes and needles.

Treatment for drug dependence is provided mainly on an out-patient basis. Many hospitals provide specialist treatment for drug misusers, mainly in psychiatric units, or have special drug treatment units. An increasing number of GPs also treat drug misusers, but only certain specialist doctors are licensed to prescribe heroin, cocaine and dipipanone (Diconal). All doctors must notify the authorities of any patient they consider to be addicted to certain controlled drugs, and guidelines on good medical practice in the treatment of drug misuse have been issued to all doctors in Great Britain. The Home Secretary has statutory powers for dealing with doctors found to have prescribed irresponsibly.

Other Sources of Provision

A number of non-statutory agencies work with and complement the health service provision. Advice and rehabilitation services including residential facilities, for example, are provided mainly by voluntary organisations. Support in the community is provided by the probation service and local social services departments.

Solvent Misuse

Action is also being taken by the Government to curb the problem of solvent misuse (the breathing in of vapour from glue, lighter fuel and other substances to achieve a change in mental state) by young people. There were 149 deaths as a result of solvent abuse in 1990. In England and Wales it is an offence to supply such substances to children under 18 if the supplier knows or has reason to believe they are to be used to cause intoxication. Government policy is directed towards preventing solvent misuse through the education of young people, parents and professionals and, where practicable, restricting the sales of solvent-based liquefied gas and aerosol products to young people. In February 1992 the Government launched a national publicity campaign on solvent misuse intended to raise parental awareness of the problem.

Smoking

Cigarette smoking is the greatest preventable cause of illness and death in Britain. It accounts for around 110,000 premature deaths and 30 million lost working days each year, and costs the NHS an estimated £500 million a year for the treatment of diseases caused by smoking (for example, heart disease, lung cancer and bronchitis). In addition, smoking by pregnant women can cause low birth weight in infants. The Government is following an active health education policy supported by voluntary agreements with the tobacco industry aimed at reducing the level of smoking.

The most recent figures show that the number of adults who smoke is continuing to fall, from 32 per cent in 1988 to 30 per cent in 1990.

Health Education

The Government aims to reduce adult smoking from 30 per cent to 20 per cent by the year 2000. A further aim is to reduce smoking by young people by one-third between 1988 and 1994. A £2 million-a-year campaign directed at those aged 11 to 15 started in late 1989 and is planned to last until 1994. In late 1991 the Government launched a £1 million campaign over two years to alert women to the dangers of smoking during pregnancy.

Education on the harmful effects of smoking is included in the National Curriculum for all pupils in publicly maintained schools in England and Wales.

The Government also supports the work of the voluntary organisation Action on Smoking and Health (ASH), whose services include a workplace services consultancy, offering advice and help to employers in formulating smoking policies. The Government is committed to creating a smoke-free environment, with facilities where appropriate for those who wish to smoke, by encouraging suitable smoking policies in public places. In 1991 it published a code of practice on smoking in public places. Health authorities have been asked to promote non-smoking as the normal practice in health service buildings and to give help and advice to people who want to give up smoking. The Independent Scientific Committee on Smoking and Health estimated that 'passive smoking', especially in the workplace and the home, may cause several hundred deaths through lung cancer every year.

Voluntary Agreements

Voluntary agreements between the Government and the tobacco industry regulate the advertising and promotion of tobacco products, and sports sponsorship by the industry. The agreement on tobacco advertising provides for the use on posters of six different health warnings about the dangers of smoking and contains measures to protect groups at particular risk, such as children, young people and women in early child-bearing years. Under the revised agreement, which came into force in 1992, new tougher health warnings now appear on tobacco advertising, and shopfront advertising is to be reduced by 50 per cent by 1996. The voluntary agreement on sports sponsorship covers levels of spending, restrictions on sponsorship of events chiefly for spectators under 18 years, and controls over the siting of advertising at televised events.

Legislative Measures

It is illegal to sell any type of tobacco product to children. Legislation introduced in 1992 has increased the maximum fine from £400 to £2,500. All tobacco advertising is banned on television and cigarette advertisements are banned on radio. In 1991 Britain voted to ban oral snuff products throughout the European Community.

Alcohol Misuse

The far-reaching effects of alcohol misuse in terms of illness, family break-ups, inefficiency at work, loss of earnings, accidents and crime are widely acknowledged. The Government considers that the reduction of such misuse requires a range of action by central and local government, voluntary and community bodies, the health professions, the drinks industry, employers and trade unions. It believes that emphasis should be placed on policies to prevent alcohol misuse and continues to seek better information about the causes of problem drinking. It also seeks to encourage healthier lifestyles, and to provide earlier help for the problem drinker.

Treatment and rehabilitation include inpatient and outpatient services in general and psychiatric hospitals and specialised alcoholism treatment units. Primary care teams (GPs, nurses and social workers) and voluntary organisations providing hostels, day centres and advisory services also play an important role.

There is close co-operation between statutory and voluntary organisations. The national voluntary agency Alcohol Concern, which is receiving a government grant of some £612,000 for 1992–93, plays a prominent role in the prevention of misuse, in training for professional and voluntary workers, and improving the network of local voluntary agencies and their collaboration with statutory bodies. In 1990 Alcohol Concern launched a workplace advisory service with initial government funding of £100,000 as part of a campaign to persuade companies that alcohol misuse is an industrial as well as a social problem. From 1990–91 to 1993–94 a total government contribution of £6 million is being allocated to Alcohol Concern for improving and extending the network of advisory and counselling services. An additional grant of £2.1 million is being paid to local authorities during 1992–93. This is to assist voluntary agencies in improving and extending residential provision for alcohol and drug misusers. The Scottish Council on Alcohol undertakes similar work in Scotland. Research and surveys on various aspects of alcohol misuse are funded by several government departments.

In 1987 the Government established an interdepartmental group to develop strategy for combating the misuse of alcohol. Measures taken include legislative changes as well as steps to secure better health education and more effective action by local services and organisations. In 1988 the law banning the sale of alcohol to people under 18 years was strengthened and stricter controls on alcohol advertising were introduced. Independent television restricts the advertising of alcohol in programmes aimed at young people.

In 1989 the Government announced increased funding for the Health Education Authority's expanded alcohol education programme. This aims to reduce the harm caused by the misuse of alcohol by promoting sensible drinking as part of a healthy way of life. It also seeks to develop a climate of opinion which favours appropriate measures to prevent alcohol-related harm. Alcohol misuse co-ordinators have been appointed in each of the 14 regional health authorities in England with the aim of developing strategies to counter the misuse of alcohol.

AIDS

The number of cases of AIDS reported in Britain continues to rise: by the end of June 1992 the cumulative total of reported cases of AIDS was 6,111, of whom 3,813 (62 per cent) had died; the cumulative total of recognised HIV infections was 17,770. Recent statistics show a steady increase in the number of AIDS cases among injecting drug users and people infected through heterosexual intercourse.

The Government Strategy

The Government has a comprehensive strategy to control the spread of HIV in Britain, and to provide diagnostic and treatment facilities, counselling and support services for those infected or at risk. The five main elements are:

—to limit the spread of HIV infection through public awareness campaigns, community-based prevention initiatives, and improved infection control procedures;

—to improve understanding of the nature of HIV infection, how it is transmitted, and how HIV-related illness can be prevented and treated;

—to provide appropriate diagnostic treatment, care and support services for those affected by HIV;

—to encourage understanding and compassion, discourage discrimination and safeguard confidentiality, within the wider context of public health requirements; and

—to foster exchange of information between countries, and to persuade against coercive and discriminatory measures.

Public Education Campaigns

The first major public education campaign on AIDS was launched in 1987, aimed at increasing awareness and knowledge and encouraging changes in behaviour. Campaigns are now administered by the Health Education Authority (see p. 45), using the mass media and supporting educational work aimed at the general public and specific sections of the population. A National AIDS helpline was established in support of the AIDS public education campaign, operating 24 hours a day. By the end of 1992–93 the Government will have allocated over £73 million to this work. National campaigns are supplemented by local HIV prevention initiatives run by health and local authorities and by the voluntary sector. Extra funds have been allocated for this work, which is led by district prevention co-ordinators. The Government continues to spend more on HIV/AIDS health education than on any other single health education programme.

A priority in 1992–93 is to ensure that health education messages reach people in black and other ethnic minority groups more effectively, and that access to services is improved.

Funding for Services

The Government continues to make additional funding available to health authorities and local authorities for treatment and advisory services, needle exchange schemes for drug misusers (see p. 34) and training staff. In 1992–93, £181.5 million is being provided to health authorities and £15.3 million to local authorities towards the costs of providing HIV-related services. Government grants of £76 million have been allocated to the Macfarlane Trust to help haemophiliacs in Britain who have become infected with HIV as a result of treatment with infected blood products. Voluntary named and anonymous screening tests for HIV began in 1990. The first results of anonymised testing carried out in sexually transmitted disease clinics and in antenatal clinics indicated a high incidence of HIV in the London area. In response to this the Government has set up an AIDS Action Group to look at, among other things, ways of improving prevention work and access to services for particular groups.

Research

The Medical Research Council's (MRC) AIDS-directed programme was founded in 1987 to develop a vaccine against HIV, and drugs to treat people infected with the virus. Government funding for the MRC's work will have amounted to £66 million by the end of 1992–93.

A new drug, zidovudine—Retrovir (AZT)—which prolongs survival in patients with AIDS and may delay disease progression in people infected with HIV, was developed by a British pharmaceutical company. The drug was licensed for use in HIV-infected individuals in 1987.

Voluntary Agencies

A number of voluntary agencies receive financial support from the Government (almost £2 million in 1992–93). Among them, the Terrence Higgins Trust, London Lighthouse and the Scottish AIDS Monitor promote knowledge about the disease and help people with AIDS and HIV. Both London Lighthouse and the

Mildmay Mission Hospital, in London, provide hospice care and community support.

International Co-operation

Britain gives high priority to international efforts to reduce the spread of HIV and AIDS. The Government fully supports the work of the World Health Organisation (WHO) in co-ordinating international action, and has committed £26 million to the WHO's Global Programme on AIDS, which is helping developing countries to establish and develop national AIDS control programmes. Britain has also pledged £8.2 million in support of WHO-co-ordinated national programmes in Commonwealth African and Asian countries and in Britain's Caribbean Dependent Territories.

Other assistance includes a grant of nearly £3 million over six years to the International Planned Parenthood Federation for AIDS-related activities; and some £3 million for research into the demographic, behavioural, social and economic aspects of AIDS in the developing world. Assistance amounting to nearly £1 million has also been provided under a joint funding scheme to British-based non-governmental organisations for small AIDS-related projects in developing countries.

Infectious Diseases

District health authorities (health boards in Scotland) carry out programmes of immunisation against diphtheria, measles, mumps, rubella, poliomyelitis, tetanus, tuberculosis and whooping cough. A combined vaccine against measles, mumps and rubella introduced in 1988 replaced that for measles for children in the second year of life. A new vaccine, 'Hib', introduced in October 1992, offers protection against invasive haemophilus disease, a major cause of meningitis in children under five years. Immunisation is voluntary, but parents are encouraged to protect their children. The proportion of children being vaccinated has been increasing since the end of 1978. In 1990 the Government introduced special payments to GPs who achieve targets of 70 and 90 per cent uptake of child immunisation. The response to these targets has been encouraging in many areas and the Government estimates that 90 per cent of GPs now earn bonus payments for meeting such targets.

The Public Health Laboratory Service provides a network of bacteriological and virological laboratories throughout England and Wales which conduct research and assist in the diagnosis, prevention and control of communicable diseases. Microbiological work in Scotland and Northern Ireland is carried out mainly in hospital laboratories.

Cancer Screening

Breast cancer accounts for some 13,000 deaths in England each year. To help combat this, the Government has set up a breast cancer screening service for all women aged between 50 and 64. The aim of the programme is to reduce breast cancer deaths among women invited for screening by 25 per cent by the year 2000. All eligible women in England and Wales should have been invited for mammography screening by March 1993 (and in Scotland and Northern Ireland by 1994).

About 1,700 women die each year in England from cancer of the cervix. The cervical screening programme aims to reduce such deaths by inviting women at risk to be screened regularly. All district health authorities in England have computerised call and recall systems, which enable all women aged between 20 and 64 to be invited regularly for cervical cancer screening. Similar arrangements apply in Wales, Scotland and Northern Ireland. Special payments are made to GPs who achieve uptake targets of 50 and 80 per cent.

Health Education

In England health education is promoted by the Health Education Authority, a part of the NHS with the major executive responsibility for public education in Britain about AIDS (see p. 40). In addition, in England the Authority's functions are to:

—advise the Government on health education;

—plan and carry out health education programmes in co-operation with health authorities and other bodies; and

—sponsor research and evaluation.

It also assists in the provision of training, and provides a national centre of information and advice on health education. Major campaigns carried out by the Authority include those that focus on coronary heart disease (represented by the Look After Your Heart initiative), smoking and alcohol misuse. The Government has allocated some £34 million to the Authority for health education in England for 1992–93.

In Wales health education is undertaken by the Welsh Health Promotion Authority. The Health Education Board for Scotland and the Northern Ireland Health Promotion Agency are responsible for health education in their areas.

Almost all health authorities have their own health education service, which works closely with health professionals, health visitors, community groups, local employers and others to determine the most suitable local programmes. Increased resources in the health service are being directed towards health education and preventive measures.

Healthier Eating

There has been growing public awareness in recent years of the importance of a healthy diet. Following recommendations issued by the Committee on Medical Aspects of Food Policy (COMA), the Government has advised people to reduce their intake of fats, particularly saturated fats, sugar and salt, since this could help to reduce the possibility of cardiovascular disease.

Nutritional labelling indicating the energy, fat, protein and carbohydrate content of food is being encouraged on a voluntary basis. Some supermarket chains have already introduced voluntary labelling schemes.

To help people reduce their fat intake, the Government has issued guidelines on the labelling of food to show nutrient content in a standard format.

Current work by COMA includes a review of the relationship between diet and cardiovascular disease; and matters relating to the nutrition of infants, children and the elderly. In 1989 the Committee issued a report on the role of dietary sugars in human disease and on the diets of schoolchildren. In 1991 it published a major report containing comprehensive information on recommended personal intakes of food energy and nutrients.

The four health promotion departments in Britain have all run public information campaigns promoting healthy eating.

Environmental Health

Environmental health officers employed by local authorities are responsible for the control of air pollution and noise, and food

Over 70 per cent of GP practices in the NHS now use computers.

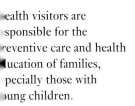

ealth visitors are
sponsible for the
eventive care and health
ucation of families,
pecially those with
oung children.

A check-up at a well-man clinic.

Hospice patient and doctor.

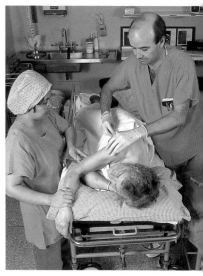

A three-year research study which aims to provide a new approach to the treatment of chronic pain began in 1992 as a collaboration between University College, London, and the Sandoz chemical company.

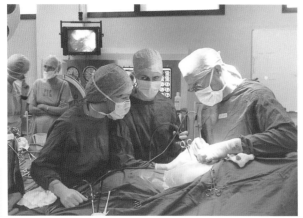

The world's first key-hole surgery on lung cancer, carried out at Broadgreen Hospital, Liverpool, in 1991.

The blood transfusion service collects over 2.3 million blood donations from voluntary unpaid donors each year.

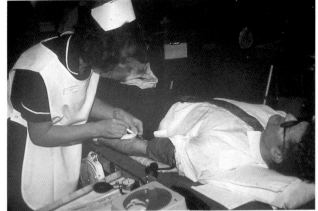

Cigarettes from each of the 150 brands on sale in Britain are tested for tar and nicotine content and for carbon monoxide at the Laboratory of the Government Chemist.

Every year members of the WRVS Food Service deliver 15 million meals on wheels and 3 million meals in luncheon clubs.

District nurses offer skilled nursing care to people at home.

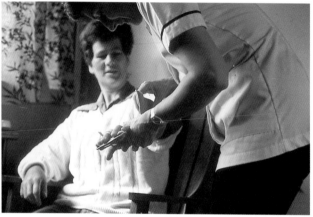

Sally and Richard Greenhill

A disabled child using ORAC, a speech communications aid developed at Leicester University.

hygiene and safety. Their duties also cover the occupational health and safety aspects of a variety of premises, including offices and shops; the investigation of unfit housing; and in some instances refuse collection and home safety. Doctors who specialise in community medicine and are employed by the health authorities advise local authorities on the medical aspects of environmental health, infectious diseases and food poisoning. They may also co-operate with the authorities responsible for water supply and sewerage. Environmental health officers at ports and airports carry out duties concerned with shipping, inspection of imported foods and disease control. In Northern Ireland district councils are responsible for noise control; collection and disposal of refuse; clean air; and food composition, labelling and hygiene.

Safety of Food

It is illegal to supply food unfit for human consumption or to apply any treatment or process to food which makes it harmful to health. Places where food or drink is prepared, handled, stored or sold must conform to certain hygiene standards. Environmental health officers may take for examination samples of any food on sale or being distributed. Special regulations control the safety of particular foods such as milk, meat, ice-cream and shellfish. The Food Safety Directorate was established within the Ministry of Agriculture, Fisheries and Food in 1989, to maintain the safety and quality of Britain's food supplies. The Directorate works closely with the Department of Health, which is responsible for the public health aspects of food safety. A consumer panel gives consumers a direct means of conveying their views on food safety and consumer protection issues to the Government.

Expert committees advise the Government on microbiological and chemical food safety, novel foods and processes, and veterinary products. The independent Advisory Committee on the Microbiological Safety of Food, for example, assesses the risks to human health from micro-organisms in food and drink and recommends action where appropriate.

The Food Safety Act 1990 emphasises food safety and consumer protection throughout the food chain. The Act applies to England, Wales and Scotland, introducing more effective powers and greatly increased penalties for offenders. Food companies must show that they have taken all reasonable precautions in manufacture, transport, storage and preparation. Special regulations govern the temperatures at which foods such as cooked meats should be stored. Separate, but similar, legislation exists in Northern Ireland.

Safety of Medicines

The health and agriculture ministers are responsible for the licensing of medicines for human and veterinary use. The Medicines Commission advises the ministers on policy. The Committees on Safety of Medicines and on Dental and Surgical Materials and on the Review of Medicines advise on the safety and quality of medicinal products for human use. Both Committees also monitor adverse reactions to drugs. Legislation also controls the advertising, labelling, packaging, distribution, sale and supply of medicinal products.

Research

In 1991–92 the Department of Health in England spent about £22.3 million on health research, in addition to expenditure by the Medical Research Council (the main government agency for the support of biomedical and clinical research). Priority areas include research into AIDS, primary health care, community care and child care, the NHS and personal social services staffing, public health and the NHS acute sector. Future priorities will take account of the *Health of the Nation* White Paper (see p. 12).

For England and Wales the Director of Research and Development at the Department of Health advises ministers on all aspects of health research. In Scotland the directly funded programme is administered by the Chief Scientist of the Scottish Office Home and Health Department.

The strategy for the NHS research and development programme aims to ensure that health service care is based on high-quality research relevant to improving the health of the nation. The programme is managed by the regional health authorities, which are developing their own research plans. It is intended that up to 1.5 per cent of NHS expenditure will be used for research and development by 1997.

The Department of Health is involved in international research and development, and takes part in the European Community's medical and public health research programme.

The Health Professions

Doctors and Dentists

Only people on the medical or dentists' registers may practise as doctors or dentists in the NHS. University medical and dental schools are responsible for teaching; the NHS provides hospital facilities for training. Full registration as a doctor requires five or six years' training in a medical school and hospital, with a further year's experience in a hospital. For a dentist, five years' training at a dental school is required. The regulating body for the medical profession is the General Medical Council and for dentists, the General Dental Council. The main professional associations are the British Medical Association and the British Dental Association.

Nurses

The minimum period of training required to qualify for registration as a first-level nurse in general or mental health, mental handicap, or children's nursing is normally three years. Midwifery training for registered general nurses takes 18 months, and for other student midwives three years. Health visitors are registered general nurses who have completed a one-year course in health visiting. District nurses are registered general nurses who practise within the community. They must complete a six-month course followed by a period of supervised practice in district nursing.

Project 2000 is a scheme to reform the education of nurses, designed to make training more attractive and to give nurses a broader based education, enabling them to work in hospitals or the community without extensive further training. In 1992–93 the Government is allocating £98 million to fund the scheme in England, where a total of 64 colleges now offer Project 2000 courses; comparable arrangements are being made in other parts of Britain. The United Kingdom Central Council for Nursing, Midwifery and Health Visiting is responsible for regulating and registering these professions.

Pharmacists

Pharmacists in general practice and in hospital must be registered with the Royal Pharmaceutical Society of Great Britain or the

Pharmaceutical Society of Northern Ireland. A three-year degree course approved by the Society followed by a year's approved training is necessary before registration. Most medicines can be supplied to customers only by, or under the supervision of, a registered pharmacist.

Opticians

The General Optical Council regulates the professions of ophthalmic optician and dispensing optician. Only registered ophthalmic opticians (or registered ophthalmic medical practitioners) may test sight. Training of ophthalmic opticians takes four years, including a year of practical experience under supervision. Dispensing opticians take a two-year full-time course with a year's practical experience or follow a part-time day-release course while employed with an optician.

Other

State registration may also be obtained by chiropodists, dietitians, medical laboratory scientific officers, occupational therapists, orthoptists, physiotherapists and radiographers. The governing bodies are seven boards, corresponding to the professions, under the general supervision of the Council for Professions Supplementary to Medicine. Training lasts one to four years and only those who are state registered may be employed in the NHS and some other public services.

Dental therapists (who have taken a two-year training course) and dental hygienists (with a training course of about a year) may carry out some simple dental work under the supervision of a registered dentist.

In 1990 a new group of NHS staff—health care assistants—began work in hospitals and the community. They are intended to support the work of more highly qualified staff.

Arrangements with Other Countries

The member states of the European Community have special health arrangements under which Community nationals resident in a member state are entitled to receive emergency treatment, either free or at a reduced cost, during visits to other Community countries. There are also arrangements to cover people who go to work or live in other Community countries. In addition, there are reciprocal arrangements with some other countries under which medical treatment is available to visitors if required immediately. Visitors are generally expected to pay if the purpose of their visit is to seek medical treatment. Visitors who are not covered by reciprocal arrangements must pay for any medical treatment they receive.

Personal Social Services

Personal social services assist elderly people, disabled people and their carers, children and young people, and families. Major services include skilled residential and day care, help for people confined to their homes and the various forms of social work. The statutory services are provided by local government social services authorities in England and Wales, social work departments in Scotland and health and social services boards in Northern Ireland. Alongside these providers are the many and varied contributions made by independent voluntary services. Much of the care given to elderly and disabled people is provided by families and self-help groups.

Demand for these services is rising because of the increasing number of elderly people and because groups such as the elderly, the disabled, and mentally ill people, or those with learning disabilities, can lead more normal lives in the community, given suitable support and facilities. The share of health authority resources devoted to community care services increased from 8.4 per cent in 1978–79 to just over 13 per cent in 1990–91.

Management Reforms

New policies on community care in England, Wales and Scotland are being implemented in stages under the NHS and Community Care Act 1990. Many of the procedures which local authorities will be implementing correspond to similar procedures being introduced in the NHS (see p. 9). Local authorities will increasingly act as enablers and commissioners of services on an assessment of their populations' needs for social care.

—Since April 1991 inspection units have been responsible for inspecting local authority as well as independent residential care homes.

—Since April 1991 local authorities have had to have procedures for dealing with complaints about their social services.

—Since April 1992 local authorities have been obliged to produce community care plans after wide consultation with the NHS and other interests.

—In April 1993 new procedures for assessing individuals' care needs and commissioning services to meet them will be introduced.

Local authorities will then become responsible for funding and arranging social care in the community. This will include the provision of home helps or home care assistants to support people in their own homes, and making arrangements for residential and nursing home care for those no longer able to remain in their own homes.

Elderly People

Between 1978–79 and 1989–90 total spending on health services for elderly people increased by 43 per cent and net spending on social services by 48 per cent in real terms. (About 5 per cent of those aged 65 or over live in residential homes.)

Services for elderly people are designed to help them live at home whenever possible. These services may include advice and help given by social workers, domestic help, the provision of meals in the home, sitters-in, night attendants and laundry services as well as day centres, lunch clubs and recreational facilities. Adaptations to the home can overcome a person's difficulties in moving about, and a wide range of aids is available for people with difficulties affecting their hearing or eyesight. Alarm systems have been developed to help elderly people obtain assistance in an emergency. In some areas 'good neighbour' and visiting services are arranged by the local authority or a voluntary organisation.

Many local authorities provide free or subsidised travel for elderly people within their areas. Social services authorities also provide residential home care for the elderly and those in poor health, and register and inspect homes run by voluntary organisations or privately.

As part of their responsibility for public housing, local authorities provide homes designed for elderly people; some of these developments have resident wardens. Housing associations and private builders also build such accommodation.

Disabled People

Britain has an estimated 6 million adults with one or more disabilities, of whom around 400,000 (7 per cent) live in communal establishments. Over the past ten years there has been increasing emphasis on rehabilitation and on the provision of day, domiciliary and respite support services to enable disabled people to live independently in the community wherever possible.

Local social services authorities help with social rehabilitation and adjustment to disability. They are required to identify the number of disabled people in their area and to publicise services, which may include advice on personal and social problems arising from disability, as well as occupational, educational, social and recreational facilities, either at day centres or elsewhere. Other services provided may include adaptations to homes (such as ramps for wheelchairs, and ground-floor toilets); the delivery of cooked meals; and help in the home. In cases of special need, help may be given with installing a telephone or a television. Local authorities and voluntary organisations may provide severely disabled people with residential accommodation or temporary facilities to allow their carers relief from their duties. Specially designed housing may be available for those able to look after themselves.

Some authorities provide free or subsidised travel for disabled people on public transport, and they are encouraged to provide special means of access to public buildings. Special government regulations cover the provision of access for disabled people in the construction of new buildings.

The Independent Living Fund was set up in 1988 to provide financial help to very severely disabled people who need paid domestic support to enable them to live in their own homes. During 1991–92 nearly 15,000 people received help from the Fund. The Fund, for which the Government is providing £77 million in 1992–93, will run until April 1993. After that people needing such help will be catered for under the mainstream arrangements for community care. In 1991 the Government committed £3 million for a pilot scheme—the national disability information project—designed to improve information services for disabled people and their carers.

People with Learning Disabilities (Mental Handicap)

The Government's policy is to encourage the development of local services for people with learning disabilities and their families through co-operation between health and local authorities and voluntary and other organisations.

Local authority social service departments are the main statutory agency for planning and arranging services for people with learning disabilities. They provide such services as short-term care, support for families in their own homes, residential accommodation and various types of day care. The main aims of the services are to ensure that as far as possible people with learning disabilities can lead full lives in their communities and that no one is admitted to hospital unless it is necessary on health grounds.

The NHS provides alternative services where the general health needs of people with learning disabilities cannot be met by ordinary NHS services, and residential care for those with severe disabilities or whose needs can only effectively be met by the NHS.

People with Mental Illness

Government policy aims to ensure that people with mental illnesses should have access to all the services they need as locally as possible. These services should be based on a comprehensive network of health and social services facilities in each district. They should be community based and easily accessible.

In England between 1981 and 1991:

—the number of community psychiatric nurses more than trebled (to 3,600); and

—places in day hospitals increased by 75 per cent (to 22,700);

Between 1979 and 1991:

—places in local authority residential homes grew by over 25 per cent (to 4,500); and

—local authority day centre places more than doubled to 15,100.

Arrangements made by social services authorities for providing preventive care and after-care for mentally ill people in the community include day centres, social centres and residential care. Social workers help patients and their families with problems caused by mental illness. In some cases they can apply for a mentally disordered person to be compulsorily admitted to and detained in hospital. The Mental Health Act Commission aims to provide improved safeguards for such patients. Similar arrangements apply in Scotland and Northern Ireland.

Since April 1991 district health authorities (health boards in Scotland) have been required to plan individual health and social care programmes for all patients leaving hospital and for all new patients accepted by the specialist psychiatric services. Other measures include a review of public funding of voluntary organisations concerned with mental health and a new grant (£31.4 million for 1992–93) to local authorities to encourage them to increase the level of social care available to mentally ill patients. A review of mental health nursing was announced in April 1992. A review of health and social services for mentally disordered offenders was completed in July 1992.

There are many voluntary organisations concerned with mental illness and learning disabilities, and these play an important role in the provision of services for both of these groups of people.

Help to Families

The Government believes in the central importance of the family to the well-being of society and considers that stable adult relationships are needed to support and enhance family life. Social services authorities, through their own social workers and others, give help to families facing special problems. This includes services for children at risk of injury or neglect who need care away from their own families, and support for family carers who look after elderly and other family members, in order to give them relief from their duties. They also help single parents. There are now many refuges run by local authorities or voluntary organisations for women, often with young children, whose home conditions have become intolerable. The refuges provide short-term accommodation and support while attempts are made to relieve the women's problems. Many authorities also contribute to the cost of social work with families (such as marriage guidance) carried out by voluntary organisations.

The Self-help and Families Project provides funding for nine voluntary agencies to assist groups of families to help themselves. The Government launched a three-year initiative in 1989 to increase voluntary sector provision in England for disadvantaged families with children under five. With funds of £2 million, it is enabling voluntary organisations to research and develop day care services, particularly for single parents and families living in temporary accommodation.

Child Care

Day care facilities for children under five are provided by local authorities, voluntary agencies and privately. In allocating places in their day nurseries and other facilities, local authorities give priority to children with special social or health needs. Local authorities also register childminders, private day nurseries and playgroups in their areas and provide support and advice services. A total of £1.5 million is to be made available to voluntary organisations over a period of three years starting in 1992, to help the development of out-of-school services.

The authorities can offer advice and help to families in difficulties to promote the welfare of children. The aim is to act at an early stage to reduce the need to put children into care or bring them before a court.

Child Abuse

Cases of child abuse are the joint concern of many authorities, agencies and professions. Local review committees provide a forum for discussion and co-ordination and draw up policies and procedures for handling these cases. The Government established a central training initiative on child abuse in 1986. This consists of a variety of projects, including training for health visitors, school nurses, and local authority social services staff. Training packs have been drawn up for those concerned with implementing the Children Act 1989 (see below).

In England, Wales and Northern Ireland children under the age of 14 in child abuse cases are able to give evidence to courts through television links, thus sparing them from the need to give evidence in open court.

Children in Care

Local government authorities must provide accommodation for children in need in their area who require it because they have no parent or guardian, have been abandoned or whose parents are unable to provide for them. The number of children in the care of local authorities continues to decline. Provisional statistics show that:

—the total number of children in care fell from 92,300 in 1981 to 59,800 in 1991;

—the number of children in care placed with foster parents increased from 39 per cent in 1981 to 57 per cent in 1991; and

—between 1990 and 1991 the number of children in residential care fell from 12,670 to under 12,000.

Under the Children Act 1989, which came into effect in England and Wales in 1991, parents of children in care retain their parental responsibilities but act as far as possible as partners with the authority. There is a new requirement to prepare a child for leaving the local authority's responsibility and to continue to advise him or her up to the age of 21. Local authorities are required to have a complaints procedure with an independent element to cover children in their care.

In England and Wales a child may be brought before a family proceedings court if he or she is neglected or ill-treated, exposed to moral danger, beyond the control of parents or not attending school. The court can commit the child to the care of a local authority under a care order. Under the Children Act 1989 certain preconditions have to be satisfied to justify an order. These are that the child is suffering or is likely to suffer significant harm because of a lack of reasonable parental care or is beyond parental control. However, an order is made only if the court is also satisfied that this will positively contribute to the child's well-being and be in his or her best interests. In court proceedings the child is entitled to separate legal representation and the right to have a guardian to protect his or her interests. All courts have to treat the welfare of the child as the paramount consideration when reaching any decision about his or her upbringing. The family proceedings court consists of specially trained magistrates with power to hear care cases as well as all other family and children's cases.

In Scotland children in trouble or in need may be brought before a children's hearing, which can impose a supervision requirement on a child if it thinks that compulsory measures are appropriate. Under these requirements most children are allowed to remain at home under the supervision of a social worker but some may live with foster parents or in a residential establishment while under supervision. Supervision requirements are reviewed at least once a year until ended by a children's hearing or by the Secretary of State. A review of child care legislation in Scotland has been conducted and its results are under consideration.

In Northern Ireland the court may send children in need or in trouble to a training school, commit them to the care of a fit person (including a health and social services board), or make a supervision order. Children in trouble may be required to attend an attendance centre or may be detained in a remand home. New child care legislation is being prepared in Northern Ireland. Where appropriate it will reflect the changes introduced in England and Wales and will make a distinction between the treatment of children in need of care and young offenders.

Fostering and Community Homes

When appropriate, children in care are placed with foster parents, who receive payments to cover living costs. Alternatively, the child may be placed in a children's home, voluntary home or other suitable residential accommodation. In Scotland local authorities are responsible for placing children in their care in foster homes, in local authority or voluntary homes, or in residential schools. In Northern Ireland there are residential homes for children in the care of the health and social services boards; training schools and remand homes are administered separately. Regulations concern–

ing residential care and the foster placement of children in care are made by central government.

Adoption

Local authorities are required by law to provide an adoption service, either directly or by arrangement with a voluntary organisation. Agencies may offer adoptive parents an allowance in certain circumstances if this would help to find a family for a child. Adoption is strictly regulated by law, and voluntary adoption societies must be approved by the appropriate social services minister. The Registrars-General keep confidential registers of adopted children. Adopted people may be given details of their original birth record on reaching the age of 18, and counselling is provided to help them understand the circumstances of their adoption. An Adoption Contact Register enables adopted adults and their birth parents to be given a safe and confidential way of making contact if that is the wish of both parties. A person's details are entered only if they wish to be contacted.

Social Workers

The effective operation of the social services depends largely on professionally qualified social workers. Training courses in social work are provided by universities, polytechnics (in Scotland, central institutions) and colleges of higher and further education. The Central Council for Education and Training in Social Work is the statutory body responsible for promoting social work training and offers advice to people considering entering the profession. A programme to introduce two-year courses leading to a new professional qualification, the Diploma in Social Work (DipSW), is being implemented.

Professional social workers (including those working in the NHS) are employed mainly by the social services departments of local authorities. Others work in the probation service, the education welfare service, or in voluntary organisations.

The Government is committed to improving social work training. In 1992–93 it is providing £29 million through its training support programme to assist local authorities to train staff; approximately 140,000 staff are expected to benefit from training, of whom nearly half work in residential care.

Voluntary Social Services

There is a long tradition in Britain of voluntary service to the community, and the partnership between the voluntary and statutory sectors is encouraged by the Government. It has been estimated that about half of all adults take part in some form of voluntary work during the course of a year. Local and health authorities plan and carry out their duties taking account of the work of voluntary organisations. Voluntary provision enables these authorities to continue the trend towards local community care rather than institutional care for elderly and for mentally ill people and those with learning disabilities. Funding voluntary organisations also provides opportunities to try out new approaches to services which, if successful, can be included in mainstream statutory provision.

Various government schemes assist almost 3,000 local voluntary projects to enable unemployed volunteers to help disadvantaged groups in the community. Voluntary organisations also take part in several other government schemes, including Employment Training and Youth Training.

Co-ordination of government interests in the voluntary sector throughout Britain is the responsibility of the Home Office Voluntary Services Unit.

Voluntary Organisations

Funding

Voluntary organisations receive income from several sources, including contributions from individuals, businesses and trusts, central and local government grants, and earnings from commercial activities and investments. They also receive fees (from central and local government) for those services which are provided on a contractual basis. Some 500 bodies receive government grants. Tax changes in recent budgets have helped the voluntary sector secure more funds from industry and individuals. The Gift Aid scheme introduced in 1990, for example, provides tax relief on gifts of more than £400 in any one year. By the end of 1991 charities had received donations of more than £150 million under the scheme and had claimed tax repayments of £50 million on them.

Employees can now make tax-free donations to charity from their earnings. The Payroll Giving Scheme provides tax relief on donations of up to £50 a month (£600 a year). Voluntary organisations benefit not only from direct donations from the private sector but also from gifts of goods, sponsorship, secondments and joint promotions.

Charities

Over 170,000 voluntary organisations are registered as charities. In England and Wales the Charity Commission gives advice to trustees of charities on their administration. The Commission also maintains a register of charities. Organisations may qualify for charitable status if they are established for purposes such as the relief of poverty, the advancement of education or religion or the promotion of certain other purposes of public benefit. These include good community relations, the prevention of racial discrimination, the protection of health and the promotion of equal opportunity. Legislation was passed in 1992 to strengthen the Charity Commissioners' powers of investigation and supervision and increase the public accountability of charities.

The Charities Aid Foundation, an independent body, is one of the main organisations that aid the flow of funds to charity from individuals, companies and grant-making trusts.

Co-ordinating Bodies

The National Council for Voluntary Organisations is the main co-ordinating body in England, providing central links between voluntary organisations, official bodies and the private sector; around 600 national voluntary organisations are members. It also protects the interests and independence of voluntary agencies, and provides them with advice, information and other services. Councils in Scotland, Wales and Northern Ireland perform similar functions. The National Association for Councils for Voluntary Service is another network providing resources, with over 200 local councils for voluntary service throughout England encouraging the development of local voluntary action, mainly in urban areas. The rural equivalent is Action with Rural Communities in England, representing 38 rural community councils.

Types of Voluntary Organisations

There are thousands of voluntary organisations concerned with health and social welfare, ranging from national bodies to small local groups. 'Self-help' groups have been the fastest expanding area over the last 20 or so years—examples include bodies which provide playgroups for pre-school children, or help their members to cope with a particular disability. Groups representing ethnic minorities and women's interests have also developed in recent years. Many organisations belong to larger associations or are represented on local or national co-ordinating councils or committees.

Some are chiefly concerned with giving personal service, others with influencing public opinion and exchanging information. Some perform both functions. They may be staffed by both professional and voluntary workers.

Personal and Family Problems

Specialist voluntary organisations concerned with personal and family problems include family casework agencies such as the Family Welfare Association, Family Service Units and the National Society for the Prevention of Cruelty to Children. They also include marriage guidance centres affiliated to Relate: National Marriage Guidance; Child Care (the National Council of Voluntary Child Care Organisations); the National Council for One Parent Families; Child Poverty Action Group, and the Claimants' Union, which provides advice on social security benefits; and the Samaritans, which helps lonely, depressed and suicidal people.

Health and Disability

Voluntary service to both sick and disabled people is given by—among others—the British Red Cross Society, St John Ambulance, the Women's Royal Voluntary Service and the National Association of Leagues of Hospital Friends. Societies which help people with disabilities and difficulties include the Royal National Institute for the Blind, the Royal National Institute for Deaf People, the Royal Association for Disability and Rehabilitation, the Disabled Living Foundation, the Disablement Income Group, MIND (National Association for Mental Health), MENCAP (Royal Society for Mentally Handicapped Children and Adults), the Spastics Society, Alcoholics Anonymous, Age Concern, Help the Aged, and their equivalents in Wales, Scotland and Northern Ireland.

Other Organisations

National organisations whose work is religious in inspiration include the Salvation Army, the Church Army, Toc H, the Board of Social Responsibility of the Church of Scotland, the Church of England Children's Society, the Church of England Council for Social Aid, the Young Men's Christian Association, the Young Women's Christian Association, the Catholic Marriage Advisory Council, the Jewish Welfare Board and the Church's Urban Fund.

Community service of many kinds is given by young people, often through organisations such as Community Service Volunteers, Scouts and Girl Guides, and the 'Time for God' scheme run by a group of churches.

A wide range of voluntary personal services is given by the Women's Royal Voluntary Service. These include bringing 'meals on wheels' to housebound invalids and old people, providing residential clubs for the elderly, help with family problems, and assistance in hospitals and during emergencies.

Over 1,300 Citizens Advice Bureaux advise people on their social and legal rights. Some areas have law centres and housing advisory centres.

The Volunteer Centre UK provides information and research on voluntary work. Its Scottish counterpart is Volunteer Development Scotland, and in Northern Ireland the Volunteer Development Resource Unit performs a similar function. There are many local volunteer bureaux, some part-time, which direct volunteers to opportunities in both the voluntary and statutory sectors.

Social Security

Nearly a third of government expenditure is devoted to the social security programme, which provides financial help for people who are elderly, sick, disabled, unemployed, widowed, bringing up children or on very low incomes.

Some benefits depend on the payment of contributions by employers, employees and self-employed people to the National Insurance Fund, from which benefits are paid. The Government also contributes to the Fund. The other social security benefits are non-contributory and are financed from general taxation; some of these are income-related. Appeals about claims for benefits are decided by independent tribunals.

Administration

Administration in Great Britain is handled by three executive agencies of the Department of Social Security:

—the Benefits Agency, responsible for paying the majority of social security benefits;

—the National Insurance Contributions Agency, responsible for handling National Insurance contributions; and

—the Information Technology Services Agency, responsible for computerising the administration of social security—once completed there will be 20,000 terminals in over 500 locations. This will enable service to the public to be improved.

The housing and community charge benefit schemes are administered mainly by local government authorities, which

Social Security Expenditure: Great Britain 1991–92

Analysis of planned expenditure 1991–92

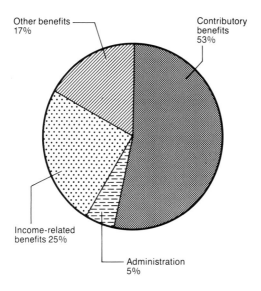

Other benefits 17%

Contributory benefits 53%

Income-related benefits 25%

Administration 5%

Percentage of expenditure by broad groups of beneficiaries 1991–92

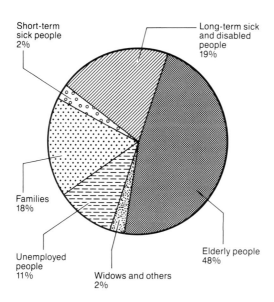

Short-term sick people 2%

Long-term sick and disabled people 19%

Families 18%

Unemployed people 11%

Widows and others 2%

Elderly people 48%

Source: *Social Security. The Government's Expenditure Plans 1992–93 to 1994–95.*

recover most of the cost from the Government. In Northern Ireland social security benefits are administered by the Social Security Agency.

Advice about Benefits

The demand for advice about benefits is partly met by the Freeline Social Security Service, which handles over a million calls each year. A complementary service, the Social Security Advice Line for Employers, handles some 2,500 calls a week. The Ethnic Freeline Service provides information on social security in Urdu, Punjabi and Chinese.

Contributions

Entitlement to National Insurance benefits such as retirement pension, sickness and invalidity benefit, unemployment benefit, maternity allowance and widow's benefit, is dependent upon the payment of contributions. There are four classes of contribution; **the rates given are effective from April 1993 to April 1994.**

—Class 1—paid by employees and their employers. Employees with earnings below £56 a week do not pay Class 1 contributions. Contributions on earnings of £56 a week and over are at the rate of 2 per cent of the first £56 of total earnings and 9 per cent of the balance, up to the upper earnings limit of £420 a week. Employers' contributions are subject to the same threshold. On earnings above the threshold, contributions rise in stages from 4.6 per cent of total earnings up to a maximum of 10.4 per cent when earnings are £195 or more a week; there is no upper earnings limit. The contribution is lower if the employer operates a 'contracted-out' occupational pension scheme.

—**Class 2—paid by self-employed people**. Class 2 contributions are at a flat rate of £5.55 a week. The self-employed may claim exemption from payment of Class 2 contributions if their profits are expected to be below £3,140 for the tax year. Self-employed people are not eligible for unemployment and industrial injuries benefits.

—**Class 3—paid voluntarily to safeguard rights to some benefits**. Class 3 contributions are at a flat rate of £5.45 a week.

—**Class 4—paid by the self-employed on their taxable profits over a set lower limit** (£6,340 a year), and up to a set upper limit (£21,840 a year) in addition to their Class 2 contribution. Class 4 contributions are payable at the rate of 6.3 per cent.

Employees who work after pensionable age (60 for women and 65 for men) do not pay contributions but the employer continues to be liable. People earning less than a certain amount do not pay contributions; neither do their employers. Self-employed people over pensionable age do not pay contributions.

Benefits

For most benefits there are two contribution conditions. First, before benefit can be paid at all, a certain number of contributions have to be paid. Secondly, the full rate of benefit cannot be paid unless contributions have been made up to a specific level over a set period. Benefits are increased annually in line with percentage increases in retail prices. The main benefits (payable weekly) are summarised overleaf (1993–94 rates).

Retirement Pension

A state retirement pension is payable, on making a claim, to women at the age of 60 and men at the age of 65. The Sex Discrimination

Act 1986 protects employees of different sexes in a particular occupation from being required to retire at different ages. This, however, has not affected the payment of state retirement pensions at different ages for men and women. The Government is committed to the equalisation of the state pension age for men and women and in 1991 published a discussion document setting out some of the issues involved.

The state pension scheme consists of a basic weekly pension of £56.10 for a single person and £89.80 for a married couple, together with an additional earnings-related pension. Pensioners may have unlimited earnings without affecting their pensions. Those who have put off their retirement during the five years after state pension age may earn extra pension. A non-contributory retirement pension of £33.70 a week is payable to people over the age of 80 who meet certain residence conditions, and who have not qualified for a contributory pension. People whose pensions do not give them enough to live on may be entitled to income support ranging from £17.30 to £23.55 a week for a single person and £26.25 to £33.70 a week for a couple. Nearly 10 million people in Great Britain received a basic state pension in 1991.

Rights to basic pensions are safeguarded for mothers who are away from paid employment looking after children or for people giving up paid employment to care for severely disabled relatives. Men and women may receive the same basic pension, provided they have paid full-rate National Insurance contributions when working. From the year 2000 the earnings-related pension scheme will be based on a lifetime's revalued earnings instead of on the best 20 years. It will be calculated as 20 per cent rather than 25 per cent of earnings, to be phased in over ten years from the year 2000. The pensions of people retiring this century will be unaffected.

Occupational and Personal Pensions

Employers are free to 'contract out' their employees from the state scheme for the additional earnings-related pension and to provide their own occupational pension instead. Their pension must be at least as good as the state additional pension. The State remains responsible for the basic pension.

Occupational pension schemes cover about half the working population and have over 11 million members. The occupational pension rights of those who change jobs before pensionable age, who are unable or who do not want to transfer their pension rights, are now protected against inflation up to a maximum of 5 per cent. Workers leaving a scheme have the right to a fair transfer value. The trustees or managers of pension schemes have to provide full information about their schemes.

As an alternative to occupational pension schemes or the state additional earnings-related pension, people are entitled to choose a personal pension available from a bank, building society, insurance company or other financial institution. By June 1992 over 4.8 million people had taken out personal pensions. A review of occupational pension law is in progress.

A Pensions Ombudsman deals with complaints about maladministration of pension schemes and adjudicates on disputes of fact or law. A pensions registry has been established to help people trace lost benefits.

Mothers and Children

Most pregnant working women can receive their statutory maternity pay directly from their employer. Statutory maternity pay is normally paid for a maximum of 18 weeks. There are two rates: where a woman has been working for the same employer for at least two years, she is entitled to 90 per cent of her average weekly earnings for the first six weeks and to the lower rate of £47.95 a week for the remaining 12 weeks; where a woman has been employed for between 26 weeks and two years, she is entitled to payments for up to 18 weeks at the lower rate.

Women who are not eligible for statutory maternity pay because, for example, they are self-employed, have recently changed jobs or given up their job, may qualify for a weekly maternity allowance of £43.75, which is payable for up to 18 weeks.

A payment of £100 from the social fund (see p. 82), may be available if the mother or her partner are receiving income support, family credit or disability working allowance. It is also available if a woman adopts a baby.

Non-contributory child benefit of £10 for the eldest and £8.10 weekly for each other child is the general social security benefit for children. Tax-free and normally paid to the mother, it is payable for children up to the age of 16 and for those up to 19 if they continue in full-time non-advanced education. In addition, one-parent benefit of £6.05 a week is payable to certain people bringing up one child or more on their own, whether as their parents or not. A non-contributory guardian's allowance of £10.95 a week for an orphaned child is payable to a person who is entitled to child benefit for that child. This is reduced to £9.80 if the higher rate of child benefit is payable for the child. In exceptional circumstances a guardian's allowance can be paid on the death of only one parent.

Child Support Agency

At present fewer than one-third of lone parents receive regular maintenance payments for their children. As part of a more general review of family justice matters, the Government is to establish a

Child Support Agency, which will take over from the courts the main responsibility for obtaining maintenance for children. The Agency will trace absent parents and collect and enforce child maintenance payments. Assessments will be made using a formula which will take into account the numbers and ages of the children and the financial circumstances of all parties. The Agency will start work in April 1993.

Widows

Widows under the age of 60, or those over 60 whose husbands were not entitled to a state retirement pension when they died, receive a tax-free single payment of £1,000 following the death of their husbands, provided that their husbands had paid a minimum number of National Insurance contributions. Women whose husbands have died of an industrial injury or disease may also qualify, regardless of whether their husbands had paid National Insurance contributions. A widowed mother with a young family receives a widowed mother's allowance of £56.10 a week with a further £9.80 for the first child and £10.95 for each subsequent child. A widow's basic pension of £56.10 a week is payable to a widow who is 55 years or over when her husband dies or when her entitlement to widowed mother's allowance ends. A percentage of the full rate is payable to widows who are aged between 45 and 54 when their husbands die or when their entitlement to widowed mother's allowance ends. Special rules apply for widows whose husbands died before 11 April 1988. Payment continues until the widow remarries or begins drawing retirement pension. Widows also benefit under the industrial injuries scheme. A man whose wife dies when both are over pension age inherits his wife's pension rights just as a widow inherits her husband's rights.

Sick and Disabled People

Statutory Sick Pay and Sickness Benefit

There is a wide variety of benefits for people unable to work because of sickness or disablement. Employers are responsible for paying statutory sick pay to employees for up to a maximum of 28 weeks. There are two weekly rates—£46.95 or £52.50—depending on average weekly earnings. Employees who are not entitled to statutory sick pay can claim weekly state sickness benefit of £42.70 instead, as can self-employed people. Sickness benefit is payable for up to 28 weeks.

Invalidity Pension and Allowance

A weekly invalidity pension of £56.10 with additions of £33.70 for an adult dependant, £9.80 for the eldest child and £10.95 for each other child is payable when statutory sick pay or sickness benefit ends. For the period to count towards receiving invalidity pension the contribution condition for sickness benefit must be satisfied. An invalidity allowance of up to £11.95 a week, depending on the age when incapacity began, may be paid, but this is offset by any entitlement to an additional invalidity pension.

Severe Disablement Allowance

A severe disablement allowance of £33.70 plus an age-related addition of up to £11.95 may be payable to people under pensionable age who are unable to work and do not qualify for the National Insurance invalidity pension because they have not paid sufficient contributions. Additions for adult dependants and for children can also be paid.

Industrial Injuries Benefits

Various benefits are payable for disablement caused by an accident at work or a prescribed disease. The main benefit is industrial injuries disablement benefit; disablement benefit of up to £91.60 a week is usually paid after a qualifying period of 15 weeks if a person is physically or mentally disabled as a result of an industrial accident or a prescribed disease. During the qualifying period statutory sick pay or sickness benefit may be payable if the person is incapable of work. The degree of disablement is assessed by a medical authority and the amount paid depends on the extent of the disablement and how long it is expected to last. Disablement of 14 per cent or more attracts a weekly pension. Except for certain progressive respiratory diseases, disablement of less than 14 per cent does not attract disablement benefit. In certain circumstances disablement benefits may be supplemented by a constant attendance allowance. An additional allowance may be payable in certain cases of exceptionally severe disablement.

Other Benefits

Disability living allowance (which replaced mobility allowance and, for people under 65, attendance allowance) was introduced in April 1992. It is a tax-free benefit with two components for people under the age of 65 who need help with personal care or with mobility. The care component has three weekly rates—£44.90, £30 and £11.95. The mobility component has two rates—£31.40 and £11.95.

An independent organisation called Motability helps disabled drivers and passengers wanting to use their higher rates of disability living allowance to obtain a vehicle.

A non-contributory, tax-free *attendance allowance* of £30 or £44.90 a week may be payable to people severely disabled at or after age 65 depending upon the amount of attention they require. People with a terminal illness receive the higher rate.

A non-contributory *invalid care allowance* of £33.70 weekly may be payable to people between 16 and pensionable age who cannot take up a paid job because they are caring for a person receiving either the higher or middle rate of disability living allowance care component or attendance allowance; an additional carer's premium may be paid if the recipient is also receiving income support, housing benefit or community charge benefit. It is estimated that some 1.4 million adults in Great Britain care for a disabled person for at least 20 hours a week.

Disability working allowance, a new tax-free benefit introduced in April 1992, provides help for disabled people in work. It is an income-related benefit payable to people working 16 hours or more a week. Awards are for fixed periods of six months. People must be receiving disability living allowance or have recently received a long-term incapacity benefit or a disability premium with an income-related benefit as a condition for receiving the new benefit. The rate payable depends on the person's income and size of family.

Unemployment Benefit

Unemployment benefit of £44.65 a week for a single person or £72.20 for a couple is payable for up to a year in any one period of unemployment. Periods covered by unemployment or sickness benefit, maternity allowance or some training allowances which are eight weeks or less apart, are linked to form a single period of interruption of work. Everyone claiming unemployment benefit has to be available for work, but unemployed people wishing to do voluntary work in the community may do so in some cases without losing entitlement to benefit. People seeking unemployment benefit are expected actively to look for work and must have good reasons for rejecting any job that is offered.

Income Support

Income support is payable to people who are not in work, or who work for less than 16 hours a week, and whose financial resources are below certain set levels. It consists of a personal allowance ranging from £26.45 weekly for a single person or lone parent aged under 18 to £69 for a couple, at least one of whom is aged over 18. Additional sums are available to families, single parents, pensioners, long-term sick and disabled people, and those caring for them who qualify for the invalid care allowance.

Housing Benefit

The housing benefit scheme assists people who need help to pay their rent, using general assessment rules and benefit levels similar to those for the income support scheme. People whose net income is below certain specified levels receive housing benefit equivalent to 100 per cent of their rent.

Both income support and housing benefit schemes set a limit to the amount of capital a person may have and still remain entitled, and any income is taken into account after income tax and National Insurance contributions.

Community Charge Benefit

The community charge benefit is a rebate scheme which offers help with the cost of the community charge to those claiming income support and others with low incomes. Subject to rules similar to those governing the provision of income support and housing benefit (see above), people can receive rebates of up to 80 per cent of their community charge. From April 1993 council tax benefit will replace community charge benefit, the maximum rebate being 100 per cent.

Family Credit

Family credit is payable to employed and self-employed working couples with children, or lone parents, with modest incomes. At least one parent must work for a minimum of 16 hours a week. The amount payable depends on a family's net income (excluding child benefit) and the number and ages of the children in the family. A maximum award, consisting of an adult rate of £42.50 weekly, plus a rate for each child varying with age, is payable if the family's net income does not exceed £69 a week. The award is reduced by 70 pence for each pound by which net income exceeds this amount. Family credit is not payable if a family's capital or savings exceed £8,000.

Social Fund

Discretionary payments, in the form of loans or grants, may be available to people on low incomes for expenses which are difficult to meet from their regular income. There are three types:

—budgeting loans to help meet important occasional expenses;

—crisis loans for help in an emergency or a disaster; and

—community care grants to help people re-establish themselves or remain in the community and to ease exceptional pressure on families.

The total discretionary budget of £340 million for 1993–94 is almost 12 per cent higher than in 1992–93.

Payments are also made from the social fund to help with the costs of maternity or funerals or with heating during very cold weather. These payments are regulated and are not subject to the same budgetary considerations as other social fund payments.

War Pensions and Related Services

Pensions are payable for disablement or death as a result of service in the armed forces or for certain injuries received in the merchant navy or civil defence during wartime, or to civilians injured by enemy action. The amount paid depends on the degree of disablement and rank held in service: the maximum disablement pension for a private soldier is £92.20 a week.

There are a number of extra allowances. The main ones are for unemployability, restricted mobility, the need for constant attendance, the provision of extra comforts, and as maintenance for a lowered standard of occupation. An age allowance of between £6.50 and £20 is payable weekly to war pensioners aged 65 or over whose disablement is assessed at 40 per cent or more. Pensions are also paid to war widows and other dependants. (The standard rate of pension for a private's widow is £72.90 a week.)

The Department of Social Security maintains a welfare service for war pensioners, war widows and other dependants. It works closely with ex-Service organisations and other voluntary bodies which give financial aid and personal support to those disabled or bereaved as a result of war.

Taxation

Some social security benefits are regarded as taxable income. Various income tax reliefs and exemptions are allowed on account of age or a need to support dependants. The following benefits are not taxable: income support (except when paid to the unemployed and to people involved in industrial disputes), family credit, attendance allowance, severe disablement allowance, industrial injuries disablement benefit, reduced earnings allowance, and war pensions. The two new benefits, disability living allowance and disability working allowance, are both tax-free.

Other Benefits

Other benefits for which unemployed people and those on low incomes may be eligible include exemption from health service charges (see p. 16), grants towards the cost of spectacles, free school meals and free legal aid. Reduced charges are often made to unemployed people, for example, for adult education and exhibitions, and pensioners usually enjoy reduced transport fares.

Arrangements with Other Countries

As part of the European Community's efforts to promote the free movement of labour, regulations provide for equality of treatment and the protection of benefit rights for employed and self-employed people who move between member states. The regulations also cover retirement pensioners and other beneficiaries who have been employed, or self-employed, as well as dependants. Benefits covered include child benefit and those for sickness and maternity, unemployment, retirement, invalidity, accidents at work and occupational diseases.

Britain also has reciprocal social security agreements with a number of other countries. Their scope and the benefits they cover vary, but the majority cover most National Insurance benefits and family benefits.

Addresses

Department of Health, Richmond House, 79 Whitehall, London SW1A 2NS.

Department of Social Security, Richmond House, 79 Whitehall, London SW1A 2NS.

Department of Health and Social Services for Northern Ireland, Dundonald House, Upper Newtownards Road, Belfast BT4 3SF.

Scottish Home and Health Department, St Andrew's House, Edinburgh EH1 3DE.

Welsh Office Public Health and Family Division, 2 Cathays Park, Cardiff CF1 3NQ.

Ministry of Agriculture, Fisheries and Food, Whitehall Place, London SW1A 2HH.

Health Education Authority, Hamilton House, Mabledon Place, London WC1H 9TX.

Health Education Board for Scotland, Woodburn House, Canaan Lane, Edinburgh EH10 4SG.

Health Promotion Agency for Northern Ireland, The Beeches, 12 Hampton Manor Drive, Belfast BT7 3EN.

Health Promotion Wales, Ffynnon Las, Ty Gles Avenue, Llanishen, Cardiff CF4 5DZ.

Health Service Commissioner for England, for Scotland and for Wales, Church House, Great Smith Street, London SW1P 3BW.

National Council for Voluntary Organisations, Regent's Wharf, 8
All Saints Street, London N1 9RL.
Public Health Laboratory Service, 61 Colindale Avenue, London
NW9 5DF.
United Kingdom Transplant Support Service Authority, South
Mead Road, Bristol BS10 5ND.

Further Reading

			£
The Government's Expenditure Plans 1992–93 to 1994–95. Department of Health and Office of Population Censuses and Statistics. Cm 1913. ISBN 0 10 119132 4.	HMSO	1992	11.55
The Government's Expenditure Plans 1992–93 to 1994–95. Department of Social Security. Cm 1914. ISBN 0 10 119142 1.	HMSO	1992	8.90
The Health of the Nation: A Strategy for Health in England. Cm 1986. Department of Health. ISBN 0 10 119862.	HMSO	1992	13.60
Scotland's Health—A Challenge To Us All. Scottish Office Home and Health Department. ISBN 0 11 494218 8.	HMSO	1992	19.50
Working for Patients. Cm 555. ISBN 0 10 105552 8.	HMSO	1989	8.80
Promoting Better Health: The Government's Programme for Improving Primary Health Care. Cm 249. ISBN 0 10 102492 4.	HMSO	1987	7.90
Caring for People: Community Care in the Next Decade and Beyond. Cm 849. Departments of Health and of Social Security, Welsh and Scottish Offices. ISBN 0 10 108492 7.	HMSO	1989	8.10

£

Report of the Committee of Inquiry into Human Fertilisation and Embryology (the Warnock Committee) Cmnd 9314.
ISBN 0 10 193140 9.   HMSO   1984   6.40

Human Fertilisation and Embryology: A Framework for the Future. Cm 259.
ISBN 0 10 102542 0.   HMSO   1987   3.30

UK Action on Drug Misuse. The Government's Strategy (Fourth edition).
ISBN 0 86252 501 2.   HMSO   1990   Free

Fourth Report of the Committee for Monitoring Agreements on Tobacco Advertising and Sponsorship.
ISBN 0 11 321436 7.   HMSO   1991   3.50

An Introduction to the Children Act 1989.
Department of Health, Lord Chancellor's Department and others.
ISBN 0 11 321254 2.   HMSO   4.95

The Individual and the Community: The Role of the Voluntary Sector.
ISBN 0 86252 699X.   Home Office   1992   Free

Cigarette Smoking 1972 to 1990. OPCS Monitor SS 91/3.   OPCS   1991   2.00

The Patient's Charter Raising the Standard.
Department of Health 1991. Available free from The Patient's Charter, Freepost, London SE99 7XU.

Annual Reports
Health and Personal Social Services Statistics for England. Department of Health. HMSO.

The Health Service in England. Department of Health, HMSO.
Health Education Authority. HEA.
Health Education Board for Scotland. HMSO.
Human Fertilisation and Embryology Authority.
Health Service Commissioner. HMSO.
Health in Scotland. The Scottish Office Home and Health Department. HMSO.
On the State of the Public Health. Department of Health. HMSO.
Social Security Advisory Committee. HMSO.
Social Security Statistics. Department of Social Security. HMSO.
Social Trends. Central Statistical Office. HMSO.

Index

Printed in the UK for HMSO.
Dd.0295731, 3/93, C30, 51-2432, 5673.